MODERN TROPICAL
GARDEN DESIGN

MODERN TROPICAL
GARDEN DESIGN

Made Wijaya

Thames & Hudson

with the influence of Zen, inspired a less-is-more movement in landscaping. The results can of course be wonderful, as we see in this book. Problems can emerge, however, when Zen-minimalist landscaping is placed alongside architecture of the same mindset, as the resulting environment can be joyless, with plants ordered up into neat rows mimicking the architectural grid, like little soldiers on a parade ground. The human element is then lost.

Made Wijaya's own garden designs celebrate the richness and variety of nature, with the added exuberance of tropical plant forms. Everything looks naturalistic but is in reality carefully orchestrated: this is not the realm of minimalism.

Two of his earlier Bali projects, both park-like in scale, at the Bali Hyatt in Sanur, and the Four Seasons at Jimbaran Bay, lead one, as all good gardens should, out of our everyday preoccupations and into a sensual, sequential world of discovery. A walk through either of these gardens from the hotel room to the café on the beach transports us on a journey in which the destination rapidly diminishes in importance. We are now fully in the present, as in a meditation. New sensations greet us at every twist of the path: an edging of sticks stuck in the ground in a criss-cross pattern has sprouted into a living fence, a pavilion is placed to offer views down onto waves rolling towards the shore, and varied masses of plantings, with much play of scale, suggest the work of a hidden choreographer (that would be Wijaya). As the path continues there is always something new and involving, and nothing repeats. These seemingly organic progressions mimic nature in the wild. However, there are underlying patterns and compositions (the hidden choreography) which, when traced back to Wijaya's original landscaping plans for these areas, relate to the cut-outs of Matisse, or the paintings of Miro and Kandinsky. And so modernism hovers just below the radar.

Hopefully this book will encourage designers to become more open to the possibilities of using nature to enhance the architecture and uplift the spirits.

FACING PAGE: A typical Geoffrey Bawa enclosed courtyard, artistically paved with a mosaic of flattish boulders. The dry garden is peopled with shapely Plumeria obtusa trees, a giant Agave and a Eucalyptus tree.

ABOVE: An antique *tempayan* pot rests in a quiet corner of The Balé, Bali.

LEFT: Moss-covered pot in a terraced courtyard at Begawan Giri Estate, Bali (now hotelier and committed modernist Christina Ong's Como Shambhala Estate). The limestone hardscape, grey volcanic walls, Dwarf Mondo Grass and feathery Fishing Pole Bamboo create an elegant ensemble.

INTRODUCTION

by MADE WIJAYA

> "Many tropical landscape designers today have lost the courage to parallel the architecture, instead they meekly add just a garnish of foliage.
> — ANNIE KELLY, decorator and author

I was never a great fan of modern gardens. What passes for 'different' or 'innovative' was, to my eye, often just architect-driven, littered with bad modern art and stiff furniture. And then I discovered the gardens of modern landscaper Jacques Wirtz in Belgium, and saw that modern gardens do not have to be like lime green Letraset. I began to look at modern tropical gardens with a more passionate eye.

There are some flavoursome alternatives, I discovered, to the rather formulaic environments being served up by many of today's trend-conscious designers. Modern gardens can be poetic and romantic, complementing and enhancing the architecture, providing a natural counterbalance to the man-made. Tropical plants not only have a place in, but often add a strong statement to, these modern gardens. These plants are not old-fashioned just because they tend to be colourful and exuberant. Young progressives need not fear the ridicule of their peers if they rejoice in nature.

As I delved further into the history of tropical landscape design, it became clear to me that 'modern' is so much more than what contemporary fashion dictates. Tropical designs with modern looks can be traced to the 1930s, and the pioneering work of Roberto Burle Marx in Brazil and Richard C. Tongg in Honolulu. Garden designers should wave wands, like Merlins of the Mulch, to soften the architecture and provide the kiss of centuries, and not just display the minimalist stamp of the 21st century.

This book takes you through my own voyage of discovery into modern tropical garden history and design, my journey from scepticism to belief. It will take you through the gardens of the early Hawaiian, Brazilian and Miami styles, through to the present-day New Asia and Zen-Modern styles, noted for their crisp vigour and startle factor. This book documents the seminal work of the early masters — Richard C. Tongg, Roberto Burle Marx, Luis Barragán, Isamu Noguchi and Geoffrey Bawa. I believe that contemporary designers will draw much inspiration from their work. This book will also introduce you to the gardens of contemporary tropical modernists. The outstanding work of garden designers Raymond Jungles of Florida, Bill Bensley of Bangkok, Martin Palleros of Perth, Karl Princic of Bali, and Ng Sek San of Malaysia, amongst many others, will be detailed and dissected. No modern plant can sleep safely in its bed.

For this book, I have chosen gardens which are artistic yet appropriate to the harsh tropical climate and to the new call for low maintenance gardens. I will illustrate my theories and choices with examples of the work of my design studio and the garden teams of the modernist architects in Singapore — the heroes of the New Asia style — and their confrères across the equatorial regions.

In matters of fashion, humans tend to be herd animals. It can be said that a few trend-setting architects — most notably Ludwig Mies van der Rohe, Frank Lloyd Wright (with his 1935 Fallingwater), and Richard Neutra — and a few talented landscape designers influenced a generation of modern tropical house and garden design. But garden design has a fashion force outside the control of the design professionals. Most gardens are designed and made by the homeowners, who take their cues from various sources — friends' gardens and garden centres, or trend books, magazines and resort hotels. Garden design is often more do-it-yourself than, say, tropical house design, where architects and developers often make most of the decisions. It is the aim of this book to provide design information and choices — drawing from the work of early modern masters as well as contemporary work from various parts of the world — and let you, the readers, decide.

FACING PAGE: Ceramic mural by Roberto Burle Marx in a garden designed by Raymond Jungles in Key West, Florida. Royal Palms, Bromeliads, and Chinese Fan Palms are scattered amongst the irregular pebble ground cover, making the poolscape look more like a Brazilian-modern water garden.

ABOVE: This garden corner in a Singapore home — with its big-format, chequered pebble-and-slate paving — was inspired by Geoffrey Bawa's Lunuganga Estate in Sri Lanka. A giant wok, surrounded by giant Bird's Nest Ferns, sits at the foot of a towering Rain Tree.

PAGE 20: Roberto Burle Marx's incredible landscape design for the Cavanellas' house in Brazil (now called 'Tacaruna' estate) — a verdant valley view is annexed as a backdrop for an ultra-modernist forecourt. Oscar Niemeyer designed the Cavanellas house.

Chapter 1

TROPICAL AMERICAS

"Havana and Rio de Janeiro practically invented tropical modern. In all its manifestations!

— TERRON SCHAEFER, style ethnographer

There is a wide variety of climates in the Americas. The tropical and subtropical area begins in the USA with Florida and Southern California, and stretches down to Mexico, Guatemala, Colombia and ends more or less in Brazil.

Tropical forests were seen by the first travellers, adventurers, conquerors and scientists as dark mysterious places brimming with unknown and potentially lethal plants and animals. However, the early indigenous Indians had a different point of view. They were dependent on the same forests for food, medicine and even decoration, as they needed flowers for their many feasts and festivals, and especially for religious holy days. Their houses reflected the climate and available materials, and were very similar to the simple village houses still common in rural Mexico and the rest of Latin America. Aztec nobles lived in houses of red or whitewashed stone which were built around central courtyards filled with flowering plants and fountains. These were perhaps the first 'designed' gardens in the Americas.

The Spanish influence in the 17th and 18th centuries formalised the gardens of Latin America and tropical USA. Town squares were planted with shady trees, and planting beds were often filled with tropical and subtropical plants recently 'discovered' in Central America. Inner courtyards were typically full of birds, practical garden plants, herbs and ornamental flowers. By the 20th century, Southern California with its subtropical climate started seeing gardens using these newly available tropical plants. Americans moving south from the colder states were inspired to create tropical paradises as a contrast to the seasonal European-style gardens they had left behind. The effect of the cool California winters and the dry climate were seemingly ignored in their enthusiasm to grow papayas, mangoes and bananas. Indoor palms and Victorian conservatories moved outside to the delight of the new settlers.

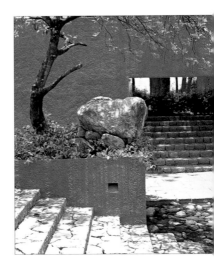

FACING PAGE: Built-in seating shaded by wooden slats in this house in Careyes, Mexico. The broad leaves of the Elephant Ear (*Alocasia*) plants contrast boldly with the striped shadows.

ABOVE: Innovative use of 'windows' in courtyard walls and bold Mexican colours by Ricardo Legorreta. The rustic limestone rubble stairs contrast with the crisp monochromatic walls.

Latin America

By the end of the First World War, fortunes were amassing in the colonial capitals of Latin America such as Mexico City and Rio de Janeiro, cities which grew to nurture some of the great garden design modernists. Modern architecture, celebrated in Central and South America, demanded modern gardens, and the striking shapes of tropical plants suited the exciting new buildings.

The first modern garden can be considered to have appeared in France, at the Exposition des Arts Décoratifs in 1925, designed by Gabriel Guevrekian who had come from the Josef Hoffmann studios in Vienna. The new principles of modern design were integrated into this garden. Plants were laid out to form abstract shapes — the garden was a sensation. The early French modernist architects, including Robert Mallet-Stevens and Le Corbusier, were inspired by this meeting of ideas.

When Le Corbusier visited Brazil in 1936, he had a profound influence on local modernist architects Lucio Costa, Oscar Niemeyer and Affonso Reidy. Brazil's Roberto Burle Marx (*profiled on page 173*), by now a landscape architect, garden designer and painter, was brought in by this influential group to design many of their gardens. The new capital Brasilia, designed by Lucio Costa, was a result of this collaboration, and became a pilgrimage destination for modernists from all over the world, much like Frank Gehry's Bilbao museum in Barcelona is today.

Roberto Burle Marx transformed his native land by replacing European-style formal gardens with native Brazilian tropical plants, and can be considered the founder of the modern tropical garden. There are more than 50,000 species of plants native to Brazil, which gave him a huge range of creative possibilities as a designer. Burle Marx's work both in tropical Brazil and in tropical climes abroad influenced garden designers all over the world: the innovative way he laid out gardens, his creative use of plants and culturally referenced accents transformed landscape design.

Garden historian Jamie James wrote: 'Nowhere on earth is nature present more powerfully than in Brazil: An irresistible tide of luxuriant rain forest flora engulfs the country's volcanic topography like a green tsunami. Yet nature met its match in a Brazilian, Roberto Burle

Chapter 2

TROPICAL ASIA

‟Modern Asian Gardens have gone the full circle since the 1950s, when concrete courts and early atomic age accents ruled. — WOFFLES WU, garden enthusiast and cosmetic surgeon

The 1930s saw many tropical Asian cities — Penang, Saigon, Mumbai, Singapore and Colombo — flirting with tropical modern Art Deco gardens. Unusual combinations of Shanghainese and European art deco touches appeared. Asian accents — such as moon windows, 'happy-lucky' multicoloured terrazzo garden benches and funky *kinchu* (Chinese vermilion) lanterns in a modern style — can be found to this day in the more sedate corners of most tropical Asian cities.

It was an exuberant, playful era for design in Asia, in step with Art Deco in Europe. South Asian countries were just emerging from centuries of colonial and horticultural oppression and Art Deco was the preferred style of these rising nationalist states. During the 19th century the stiff rule of the European overlords had its parallels in the tight municipal gardens of the colonial hill stations, with their herbaceous borders, plaster bambis and rose beds. This rather rarefied garden design tradition still enjoys a substantial following, mind you, in present-day Kuala Lumpur, Yangon, Jakarta, and the gardens of the armed forces in Chennai.

In the late 1950s, the Singapore government commissioned a public swimming pool and garden in Chinatown which experimented with the *peranakan* (Straits Chinese) love for the multihued, and also with the strict, geometric architectural shapes of Art Deco. Indonesia too developed an indigenous Deco style in the West Java capital of Bandung, the 'garden city'. The city's elite started building Art Deco villas in the Dago District, replete with black reflecting ponds, mono-planting, geometric lines, and screamingly loud landscape murals which featured local motifs and legends. Art Deco was never totally successful in the tropics, however. The exuberance of the tropical landscape tended to take over and smudge the clean lines.

By the 1950s, Southeast Asian cities were flirting with Hawaiian-style gardens in their hotels, and Brasilia-style public parks. Honolulu-based landscape architects Belt Collins did most of the early modern gardens of Singapore, Penang, Kuala Lumpur and Manila.

FACING PAGE: New Asia minimalist garden designed by P.T. Wijaya for a house in Singapore. The architecture is complemented by a lantern (inspired by an outdoor heater), the Buddha's Belly Bamboo (*Bambusa tuldoides* 'Ventricosa'), a courtyard favourite, and the *Jatropha pandurifolia* (on the right).

ABOVE: A Japanese Sago Palm (*Cycas revoluta*) in a classical Vietnamese planter.

Pete Wimberly's office, by then Wimberly, Allison Tong & Goo (W.A.T.G.), was responsible for most of the influential resort architecture of this era, most famously the Singapore and Penang Shangri-La hotels. Suddenly coconut palms and bougainvilleas were in fashion where Norfolk Island pines and dwarf ixoras had reigned supreme for decades. Fussy herbaceous borders were replaced with the more stoic mass planting of the Hawaiian modernists. Social Realist art from Mumbai, Saigon, Manila and Yangon supplanted European marble busts, wrought-iron fixtures and terrazzo-art garden furniture.

It was not until the emergence of Bali Resort Style in the 1970s — with the Bali Hyatt in Sanur and The Oberoi Bali in Legian — that a Southeast Asian regional style really took off. These Bali resort gardens were Balinese in their artwork accents and pavilions but basically planted in the English tradition of the artful natural. They were to influence the tropical garden design world for the next twenty years. They were modern in the way that Roberto Burle Marx's gardens were modern, that is, the space planning was modern, but the high notes were poetic in the romantic vein. Ruinscapes with Balinese gates, spouts, pavilions and statuary were prevalent (see my earlier book, *Tropical Garden Design*, for a more complete picture).

By the early 1990s, 'Bali' meant 'business'. Many Singapore-based landscape architects — notably Bill Bensley, Colin Okashimo, and Karl Princic — left their successful Singapore offices to enter the lucrative Bali Style stakes. They mixed Hawaiian modern leanings with a style more Asian and sensual.

Bill Bensley's work in Thailand and the Indian Ocean, notably the successful Four Seasons Resort in Chiang Mai, and The Oberoi in Mauritius, represents an apotheosis of the Bali and Hawaiian modern styles. He absorbed the decorative accents of a hundred tropical cultures — among them Burmese, South Indian, Maldivian, Timorese, Fijian, Hainanese, Javanese — and poured them all out in a raucous symphony of landscape design excess.

By the late 1990s, South Asia's modern architects — particularly those influential architects in the region's big capitals — were tired of the resort-inspired garden clichés springing up everywhere. The new generation started looking to Berlin, and not Bali. And thus the New Asia and Zen styles were born.

FACING PAGE: This Singapore garden features Tamil Nadu stone temple columns (as artworks) in a lotus pond. The water garden appears linked to the swimming pool via a stepped water cascade (not visible).

ABOVE: This stunning parkland pool by Geoffrey Bawa's protégé Channa Daswatte has the Bawa feel. It is modern, but set, effortlessly, in a natural setting.

BELOW: A typical Vietnamese Art Deco garden with plum green *Rhoeo* plants in the foreground. Most tropical Vietnamese homes have charming outdoor living rooms full of garden decorative elements — such as lanterns, bonsais on stands, and well-maintained plants.

New Asia

In the early 1960s, Geoffrey Bawa (*profiled on page 167*) of Sri Lanka developed a signature modern style based on traditional Asian courtyard architecture. The style was based on local culture, colours, interior design and landscape design traditions. It was a huge success, mostly because Bawa was a landscape artist as well as an architectural genius. His architecture was full-blooded, in a Ceylonese colonial way, but with crisp lines and modernist space planning. His gardens were fully tropical and romantic in the Italian and English traditions. The furniture and art in Bawa's larger gardens were sometimes modern but the effect was more artful-natural, Reptonesque even, than Roberto Burle Marx. His courtyards were a wonderful mix of the natural and the man-made — Asian man-made, generally.

During the 1990s, the tropical Asian region was swamped with Bawa-inspired hotel gardens, often termed 'New Asia' style. A hundred books would not have been written without Geoffrey Bawa, or without Bali-inspired gardens for that matter. Just as Bali became the world's biggest exporter of landscape tack, so too the Colombo to Galle coast became a wonderland of Bawa resort hotels.

Sadly, the generation of excellent architects Bawa inspired were not great garden-makers, though most were garden lovers. Rare is the New Asian architect who can relax his guard enough to let in a landscape artist to help caress and soften the lines of their often stunning modernist architecture.

There are many notable exceptions — Kerry Hill Architects' The Datai in Langkawi and Alila Manggis (formerly The Serai) in Bali; Kerry Hill's The Chedi Chiang Mai with landscape architect Martin Palleros; and Antony Liu's The Balé in Bali with landscape architect Karl Princic. All these gardens had lean and mean courtyards with limited decorative accents. Planting schemes, where they existed, were bold and striking.

Not surprisingly, many of these young modernist architects — Chan Soo Khian, Wong Mun Summ, and Cheong Yew Kuan — were Malaysians. Malaysia, like Colombo, had excellent modern architecture in the 1960s complemented by admirable English-Artful-Natural-Tropical modern gardens and modernist landscape lighting.

FAR LEFT: The cutting edge of New Asia: Buddhas by the truckload!

LEFT: The main pool of the minimalist-modern Sala Samui Resort & Spa, Koh Samui, Thailand.

ABOVE: The main courtyard of the Ministry of Foreign Affairs in Singapore designed to the theme 'Coastal Cultures of South East Asia'. The style is primitive-modern which complements the rather austere granite architecture.

FACING PAGE: Pared-down orientalism? A faux openwork stone panel in the bathroom court of a home in Malaysia. The soft tree ferns seem to whisper in the breeze.

Zen-Modern

The exquisitely serene Zen Buddhist gardens of monastic Japan were once known only to landscape aficionados and a few art experts. They are created by Zen Buddhist monks who, after decades of meditation, go in search of the perfect rock to place in the minimalistic but splendidly artful garden courtyards of Zen Buddhist monasteries. Perfect moss, raked sand and handsome courtyard walls complemented these rock-garden compositions. And then came the 1960s. Everything Buddha-ist was up for grabs. (See Gita Mehta's 1973 book *Karma Cola* and the 1999 strangerinparadise.com essay 'Diet Karma Cola'.)

By the late 1990s, the concept of Zen — long since distorted to mean the bland and the bloodless — reached the Malay archipelago as Zen-Modern and a pandemic broke out. Soon bulldozers were razing the ancestors' parklands in the name of Zen (young Asian urbanites had been looking for an excuse) and the artful-natural Asian garden was placed on the endangered species list. Those landscape designers who stood defiantly against this Age of the Machines (think *Terminator 3*) suddenly found themselves with a considerably diminished workload.

Thus rose the age of Zen-Modern in Southeast Asia and beyond. A wave of brilliant Kerry Hill acolytes — led by the talented duo Wong Mun Summ and Richard Hassell (WOHA) entered the design marketplace. Zen Warriors extraordinaire, they inspired a decade of architectonic gardens in Southeast Asian cities. Exuberant or artful nature was decreed old-fashioned. Ethnic art was deemed 'too ethnic' or 'spooky'. And Singapore's upbeat designers found a style — not foreign, but not too close and clammy and high-maintenance either (like the Balinese or resort styles) — that they could hang their hopes on. The Zen-Modern gardens of the early 21st century, it must be said, were architect-driven. It was a style of garden that did not require garden designers, or even gardeners!

Unlike true Zen gardens — which are the result of years of meditation and a long search for the perfect rock — the Zen-Modern garden as we know it today tends to look drawing-board derivative.

There are some warm-blooded examples, though, and it is those that I have chosen to highlight in this section. The work of Argentinean architect Martin Palleros (*profiled on page 185*) in Singapore and Bangkok, Karl Princic (*profiled on page 183*) in Bali, and Ng Sek San (*profiled on page 189*) in Malaysia, in particular, are praiseworthy. These three designers are all plant-lovers who love to do architectonic gardens, of which the strong, simple-lined Zen-Modern is the most extreme.

These three designers, whose Zen-Modern work is exemplary, come from different backgrounds — Princic from the Hawaiian school, Sek San from the Malaysian naturalist school, while Palleros emerged from a longish stint in planning and architectural design. The careers of all three crested with New Asia-style architecture.

New Asia-style gardens — with their water bodies and pared-down softscapes 'Bali-lite' — were moving towards a sleeker, more urban look. These three designers took that look, and created a brave new Asia. Their edgy hardscapes were generally balanced with small-leafed trees such as tropical eucalypts, leopard trees, and caesilpinias which provided a light, airy counter-balance. The results were crisp and refreshing, in a controlled New Asian way.

FACING PAGE AND ABOVE: Karl Princic's lean and mean landscape for The Balé, Bali. The alleyways combine architectonic space planning with tons of limestone walls and acres of wild grasses. The whole mix makes for a sleek, edgy environment.

ABOVE AND RIGHT: Modern figurative accents blend beautifully into Elisabeth Mamatis' garden in Byron Bay, New South Wales, Australia, whether it is a bronze sculpture by Erika Mayer (above) or an elegant pair of busts by Elisabeth herself (balanced by a palm grove, with the red *Clivia* providing extra touches of colour).

PAGE 64: Waving the wizard's wand — a water garden by Dean Herald at his own house in Sydney. Strong architectural elements are softened by artful natural planting. The mixture of grasses, ferns and *Ophiopogon* balances the rectilinear hardscape and dramatic water features.

CHAPTER 4

DESIGNING MODERN GARDENS

'God almighty first planted a garden and indeed it is the purest of human pleasures. It is the greatest refreshment to the spirits of man without which building and palaces are but gross handyworks.
— FRANCIS BACON

Gardens must be put together from parts — pieces of hardscape (paths, ponds, pergolas), areas of softscape (plants), and appropriate artwork and furniture accents. The result should look well balanced as between the natural and the man-made.

The last decade has seen architectural gardens become ultra-fashionable in the tropical world. Modernism has come to be equated with minimalism.

Reflecting bodies of dark water have replaced joyous water gardens. Planting schemes have become a tad monotonous and architectural — rows of spiky things, such as Spanish Bayonets (and other yuccas), dracaenas, and the ubiquitous Horsetail plant have become *de rigueur*. The same goes for colour schemes, where palettes of grey and other neutral tones have become the norm. In hardscape, man-made has started to look machine-made. Stripes of different coloured stone have become status symbols.

There are few Roberto Burle Marxes, Luis Barragáns and Geoffrey Bawas — masters at balancing landscape with architecture — among today's modernists. 'Architects all over Asia have taken over from garden designers in a sapless *coup d'état*,' one garden wit commented. Many of these gardens look as if they were designed to a formula, so indistinguishable are they from each other.

How best to counteract this? 'It's the garden designer's first job to soften the architecture, then it's the architect's job to stay inside,' quipped the same wit.

Great modern gardens combine structure and geometry with softer elements such as plants, and more dynamic elements such as art and innovative use of colour and lighting. The garden is today an extension of the living room, a space designed for outdoor entertainment and leisure. The best gardens are also comfortable, relaxing spaces designed for people, rather than indulgent exercises in hardscape excess.

The lesson I hope to impart in this chapter is: one can achieve a modern look without the garden looking either homogenised, soul-less, bird-less or god-less.

FACING PAGE: Light garden furniture adds a modern accent to this side terrace in a Singapore home.

ABOVE: The alleyways of The Balé in Bali are architectonic and sculptural. The borders of soft grasses add colour, and balance the hard lines.

Courtyards & Patios

BELOW: A charming, shady patio at La Casa Que Canta in Ixtapa, Mexico. The strong geometric paving patterns and architectural steps give this classic Hispanic courtyard a modern twist.

FACING PAGE: In his house in Mexico, architect Duccio Ermenegildo separated the outdoor living and dining areas from the rest of the garden with a series of arches. He designed the dining table and chairs to blend with the architecture.

Modern house designs often consist of a series of interlocking spaces — indoor and outdoor. These spaces are either central, like the patios or cloistered central courts of Spain which are fully enclosed, or attached to the main structure as is the case with garden terraces or roof terraces.

In ultra-modern architecture — the architecture of Luis Barragán in Mexico and Chan Soo Khian in Singapore, for example — garden courtyards are often defined by walls, or the 'wings' of the architectural courts, thus becoming outdoor living rooms with feature walls. The series of courts become compounds, a term derived from the Malay word *kampung*, meaning a group of dwellings in a village-like cluster, often walled.

Traditionally, patios — the Spanish kind — have a fountain or water feature. Similarly, reflecting bodies of water and water spouts are often woven into the fabric of contemporary architecture and its external courtyards. These water spouts are often realised in modern materials such as stainless steel and high-density ceramic which can look jarring if not pitched just right.

Peopling a courtyard with potted plants and garden furniture makes a court cosy. However, too much and the garden architecture loses its modernist edge. Popular wisdom has it that a striking exterior architecture needs a bolder planting scheme or mass planting to balance. Advice: the choice of planters, light fixtures and garden furniture must take into consideration the character of the courtyard walls and softscape elements.

Dan Kiley's courtyards at the Four Seasons Hotel Miami (*see picture on page 103*) are a good example of balancing landscape elements into a well-composed modern environment. Likewise, the courtyards and patios in Geoffrey Bawa's work are peopled with light, quirky modern garden furniture. Hawaiian modernists, on the other hand, tend to prefer heavy furniture (of the Summit furniture variety) in their lanai-style courts. This chunkiness matches the solid appearance of their pergolas, light fittings and planters.

FACING PAGE: Pond and outdoor shower overlooked by a pavilion at Begawan Giri Estate, Bali (now Como Shambhala Estate).

RIGHT, ABOVE: The Bulgari Bali — a dramatic villagescape of beautifully proportioned pavilions.

RIGHT, BELOW: A light pavilion and geometric hardscape forms blend seamlessly into this Thai riverside landscape in Kanchanaburi, Thailand.

Pavings

ABOVE: A ribbon of stone pavers and a carpet of white pebbles create a graphic modern statement.

FACING PAGE: A secret path designed by Raymond Jungles to complement the modern architecture of this house in Naples, Florida.

In the words of landscape designer, Doyan Kenti-Brown, 'A plethora of natural stone finishing can be tense-making to all but roller-derby enthusiasts.' Ludwig Mies van der Rohe's garden for the German Pavilion at the 1929 World's Fair in Barcelona was the prototype for one type of modern garden — a garden with lots of paved areas, a sleek Mondrian painting on its back — controversial at the time, but later much-copied.

In Marc Treib and Dorothée Imbert's *Garrett Eckbo: Modern Landscape for Living* (1997), there is an image of a swimming pool in a large backyard garden in suburban Los Angeles. A young boy plays the guitar at the end of a diving board, while a pretty girl watches from across the pool, leaning on the chrome pool ladder. The scored concrete pool deck is vast and merciless. There is no shade or furniture in sight. It is the 1950s' idea of modernism — gardens designed for industrial cleaning. The garden was controversial at the time but much copied. Comic films were made — most famously *Mon Oncle* (1958) starring Jacques Tati, and *The Party* (1968) starring Peter Sellers — which poked mild fun at these fully paved 'modern' gardens. Bollywood movie sets also seem to be descended from this 'All hardscape, All girls, All dancing' school of thought. It

should be noted here that, in India, the best landscape modernists all work for Bollywood! In Southeast Asia in the 1990s, tropical architectural gardens became ultra-fashionable and a tad formulaic. Modern gardens need not be hard gardens. The human eye prefers to fall on softer shapes; and ground covers, shrubs and vines can be used to comfort and caress the sharp corners and lines of elements such as planter boxes and path edges.

When laying paving stones, the pattern is important. Too complicated a design makes for a busy landscape, and can lead to edges and copings looking too garish when a simpler look is desired. Larger tiles and stone pieces help to create a more seamless look but make a space look industrial. As always, proportion is important. And this applies particularly to coping elements such as pond and planter box edges, and stair treads — too thick and it can look bulky, but too thin can look mean.

Simple cement finishes are found all over the modern gardens of South India and Sri Lanka, either brushed, scored or polished. And they always look and feel cool. The Brazilian and Mexican modernists — and thus the Miami acolytes — are doing very interesting work with concrete finishes, as are many architects and landscapers in India.

An array of paving solutions, which are exemplary not just for their innovative ways with materials and design, but also for their integration with architecture and landscape. The one above, for example, is made of marble pieces (left over from the interior contracting job), and pebblewash grout. Wall art by Bruce Goold adds modern flair to a traditional Indian tea lawn.

The architecture of Geoffrey
Bawa's Lighthouse Hotel in Sri
Lanka (above) is handsome
enough to support minimalism in
the landscape. The picture at
top left shows Bawa's ingenious
criss-cross ramp design at the
same hotel.

FACING PAGE: New Delhi landscape architect Professor Shaheer designed this constructivist paving pattern for The Park Hotel in Visakhapatnam, India.

ABOVE: Picture far left shows a neat suspended timber and metal mesh pathway through a wild tropical garden. Next to it are: detail of pebblewash paving, a meandering path with a rubble finish, and a mosaic of granite pieces.

BELOW: Coralstone, keystone (fossilized coral reef), limestone and caprock have textures and colours which are very flattering to tropical gardens. This stunning Florida garden has a coralstone path and coral 'gravel' drive.

Water Features

Bodies of water, reflecting ponds, wet walls and architectural spouts are a pretty feature of modern tropical gardens worldwide.

The three Bs — Bawa, Barragán and Burle Marx — all used water gardens and features extensively in their landscape designs. Bawa's lobby ponds at the Bentota Beach Hotel in Sri Lanka, Barragán's big U-shaped spouts, and Burle Marx's bold pond planting and primitive-modern artwork accents influenced a generation of architects and landscape modernists.

Natural water gardens are a big part of the Hawaiian modern look and provide a refreshing counterpoint to stiff modern architecture.

Today's tropical modernists tend to favour clean reflecting bodies of water — and not water gardens with a more natural look — like the design for the Tirtha Uluwatu wedding complex in Bali (*see picture on page 102*). These tend to be combined with the floating pavilion, a recurring theme in tropical landscape design.

Water bodies — clean or full of plants — can be a practical addition to any garden. Water bodies cool areas by refrigeration, that is, through the movement of air over water. They help to define areas and provide security.

When creating water bodies near architecture, it is important that the size and shape of the ponds or pools match the scale of the architecture, or one may end up with a 'poodle in a puddle' effect, that is, a water body that looks more like a mini moat or gutter than a pond.

We should remember that water bodies can be used to good effect to reflect forms in the daytime, and artificial light or moonlight at night, and we should design with an eye to where and how these reflections fall.

Water spouts are another popular design feature in modern gardens. Water falling into water feels soothing. Also, spouts, decorative and otherwise, provide trickle or splash sounds which mask traffic noise.

U-section spouts can be found everywhere, but this is one area in which I have always felt that modern garden designers could be more adventurous. Rather than always going for the same spout design, they should look to the plethora of extraordinary spout shapes found in traditional Asian architecture for inspiration.

FACING PAGE: Low tufty grass, native Florida shrub trees, Silver Buttonwood (*Conocarpus erectus 'seiceus'*) and Florida limestone pavers make a natural counterpoint to this spouting modern feature wall.

BELOW: Clever terraced water feature cum playground at the Sibu Lake Garden, Malaysia.

ABOVE LEFT: Clever concrete stairs
to pool are cantilevered off a
house wall in this Careyes,
Mexico home.

ABOVE RIGHT: Legoland meets
Aquaworld — coloured tiles are
combined to create a bold
graphic statement.

FACING PAGE: The startlingly bold
wall colour balances beautifully
with the pool in this Ricardo
Legorreta-designed house in
Napa Valley, California.

FACING PAGE: Jamie Durie of PATIO Landscape Architecture and Design likes to blur the boundary between industrial art and garden design. This showpiece garden has innovative slatted-timber stepping stones which suggest the giant leaves of the Amazonian Water Lily (*Victoria regia*).

ABOVE: Dramatic but tranquil spa courtyard at The Park Hyatt, Dubai.

RIGHT: Dark volcanic stone from Indonesia has become synonymous with modern tropical gardens throughout the world.

FAR RIGHT: Subtle submarine bubbler fountain, part of the poolscape seen on page 8.

Pools

BELOW: This pool overflow drain with a stylish, arty look uses hand-glazed tiles from Thailand (a popular choice in the design marketplace).

FACING PAGE: A large angular reflecting pond with bold concrete-edge detail on the top level of Geoffrey Bawa's highlands-tropical Kandalama Hotel in Sri Lanka.

The last twenty years have seen huge strides in tropical pool design. The infinity edge pool, where the water tumbles over the pool edge, first used by landscape designers in Acapulco in the 1950s, but made world-famous by architect Peter Muller in his pool design for the Amandari hotel in Bali in 1989, has become a tropical garden staple.

Since the Amandari pool revelation, architect Kerry Hill has done a fabulous poop-deck-into-the-jungle pool at The Chedi (now the Alila Ubud) in Bali (*see picture on page 95*) and designer Ed Tuttle has done an equally revolutionary pop-up (melting ice cube look) pool at the Amanjiwo hotel in Central Java. The idea of the swimming pool connecting almost seamlessly to a water garden — done at the Villa Bebek in Bali in 1986 and at the Sala Samui Resort & Spa in Koh Samui in 2004 — has been much copied throughout the tropical world.

Water bodies can often come as reflecting bodies (especially in the work of landscape architects such as Martin Palleros when working with architects such as Kerry Hill) which are adjacent to the architecture and designed to throw dancing shadows on the water.

American landscape legend, Dan Kiley, in his work on the pool deck at the Four Seasons Hotel in Miami, chose to make one of the swimming pools into a maze-like corridor of islands — packed with crinum lilies and love donuts — aligned diagonally to the main axis of the garden (*see picture on page 103*). His cosy but modernist outdoor sitting rooms for the same garden all lie in the 'shadow' of a six-metre-high wall of moving water which chills even as it animates the yucca- and ixora-strewn plaza-ettes.

The style and colour of pool tiles have also gone through a radical rethink over the past twenty years. Gone is the old faithful, the aqua blue. In its place many pools now have darker tiles (which tend to be warmer, be warned). Blue-green and black are popular with contemporary tropical architects, in either glass mosaic or slate. Many designers experiment with different pool looks in their homes. Fashion designer Milo did a pool in Bali in 2004 using glass bricks as tiles. The end result resembles mother of pearl. Many Hawaiian modernists

FACING PAGE: This pool provides a peaceful focus for the Sally Hirschberger hair salon in West Hollywood, California.

LEFT: Detail of pool paving (top); and swimming pool for the award-winning Mont'Kiara Damai condominium in Malaysia.

ABOVE: These violet extra-wide *chaises longues* make for dramatic accents at the pool of the Ritz Carlton Hotel, Bali.

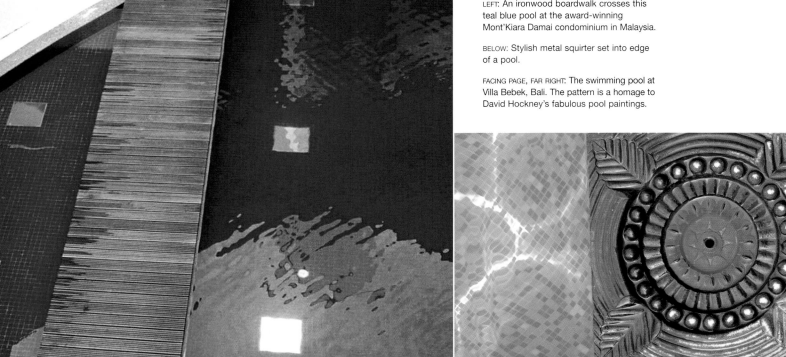

ABOVE: Underwater mural by artist David Hockney at the Roosevelt Hotel in Hollywood. Patterns on pool tiles are a design trick as old as Egypt; they can give a bland poolscape a striking twist.

LEFT: An ironwood boardwalk crosses this teal blue pool at the award-winning Mont'Kiara Damai condominium in Malaysia.

BELOW: Stylish metal squirter set into edge of a pool.

FACING PAGE, FAR RIGHT: The swimming pool at Villa Bebek, Bali. The pattern is a homage to David Hockney's fabulous pool paintings.

ABOVE: The Tirtha Uluwatu wedding complex in Bali.

RIGHT: The Balé in Bali is crisscrossed with cooling water bodies, cascades and rills.

LEFT: This swimming pool is in the central courtyard of a Singapore home. It cools the colonnades and acts as a water garden.

ABOVE: This pool, designed by American landscape legend Dan Kiley for the Four Seasons Hotel Miami, is shaded by a grove of Florida Royal Palms (*Roystonea elata*) and white Crinum Lily (*Crinum asiaticum*).

Walls

Feature walls were a big part of 1950s architectural design and interior decoration. Famed architect Richard Neutra invented the stone indoor-outdoor feature wall for his 'Californian bungalow' look. The stone wall dissected the main volumes of the house, and connected with the outdoor spaces of rambling natural gardens. Neutra used soft, rough-plaster finishes, however, for his other hardscape elements. Neutra-designed houses were always harmonious with nature and well-balanced.

Good designers tend to contrast vertical elements of the hardscape (walls, planter boxes) with horizontal elements (paths, pavings), either texturally or tonally. If the courtyard is of grass, for example, then a granite rubble wall can look striking, and not over-balance the composition towards the man-made. If the paving is crazy-pattern splitstone, for example, then a softer, cleaner, plaster-finish wall looks best.

The masters of landscape modernism used natural stone finishes where practical, and also for dramatic effect. Stone may be readily available in today's landscape marketplace but is best used sparingly — for edges, stair treads, and entertainment areas. The colour and finish (rubble-finished, split-finished, flame-finished, honed or polished) should be chosen to match the garden design so that the all-important balance of form, texture and space can be achieved.

The modern architects of Mexico City, in particular, do amazing things with volcanic stone in garden walls, continuing a 3000-year-old tradition. Dark andesites, laid as large-format stone mosaics, can be found in many gardens and public parks.

One French botanist reinvented the garden wall. Patrick Blanc was an internationally celebrated tropical botanist long before his 'Vertical Walls' came on the scene. Faced with an increasingly ugly, green-free cement jungle, Blanc invented a 'plant bed' which could cover virtually any wall. By carefully arranging a palette of plants on that bed, the French artist was then able to create a rich variety of images. The resulting floral tapestries are reminiscent of the jungle themes in the artwork of French modernist master Henri Rousseau.

FACING PAGE: The harsh light of the tropics makes for dramatic shadows on garden walls. Softer walls make for more romantic shadows.

BELOW: Spiky plum-coloured *Dracaena marginata* contrasts with the organic shapes of this rubble wall.

The placement, size and treatment of courtyard and boundary walls are of major importance in landscape design. The use of attractive walls rather than herbaceous borders to define space — in the tradition of Japanese and Chinese gardens — is a popular ploy in modern landscape design. Bathrooms with courtyard gardens attached are now a staple of the modern tropical house style.

In Asia, striking boundary walls, of a certain height, have replaced the friendly see-through fence or low boundary hedge which is still common in Honolulu, Miami, and tropical Australia. This creates a rather severe and cluttered streetscape — as walls rarely match — which is sad. Too often the wall and gate, generally designed by the architect, do not gel with the landscaper's concept. This kind of discord is to be avoided. All wall and gate design in garden areas should harmonise with the architecture of the house, and also fit in with the landscape scheme.

ABOVE: A sliver of mirror along a colonnade wall reflects the courtyard garden at the Uma hotel in Ubud, Bali.

FACING PAGE: Ingenious plaster finish on a courtyard wall created by running saw teeth along drying plaster; and, at top right, artwork niches in a coral garden wall at the Cafe Batujimbar in Bali.

PAGE 108: Rough-finished beige granite, immaculately laid, is popular in Singapore house design. Darker plants like this *Raphis excelsa* look best against lighter walls. See page 103 for another view of this house.

PAGE 109: The courtyard of a house in California designed by Koning Eizenberg with wall planes separated by colour.

FACING PAGE: The dramatic flower of the Bird-of-Paradise (*Strelitzia*) is synonymous with the tropical look. It is in fact a desert plant.

RIGHT: These black-stemmed Alocasia look great against a terracotta brick wall.

BELOW: Crinkle-cut leaf of the slow-growing *Johannesteijsmannia* palm.

ABOVE: Nancy Goslee Power's clever use of cycads in terraced planter boxes creates a wild tropical Brazilian jungle feel in this garden corner of the Norton Simon Museum in Pasadena.

LEFT: A corner of the Central Park of Lotusland, Montecito, California, with its incredible cactus, bromeliads and Spanish moss look.

FACING PAGE: This Brazilian ranch style home has a pool court designed by Roberto Burle Marx. His fascination with geometric patterns in the tropical landscape is on display here. The architecture is by Oscar Niemeyer.

LEFT: Palms jutting out from the grass, or from a homogeneous ground cover like the ophiopogon in this photo, is always a good look.

BELOW: Singapore-based designer Chang Huai-Yan adds a modernist touch to this betel nut palm forest with a sculpture of a large bird.

FACING PAGE: A classic corner by maestro-modernist Jacques Wirtz.

Colours

The tropics have always been associated with vibrant colour — look at the classical temple architecture of South India or Bali, for example, or the gardens of Fiji, Hawaii or Guatemala. In the modern era, artists such as Pierre Bonnard, Paul Gauguin and Henri Rousseau used tropical colours in their art with striking success. In architecture, Le Corbusier in his South Indian work in the 1930s, Luis Barragán in Mexico, and Geoffrey Bawa in Sri Lanka, all used broad swathes of bright tropical colour in their work. In modern interior design, one thinks of cities such as Miami, Havana and Mexico City for fabulously colourful interiors.

Over the past decade a colour-blindness has crept into architectural and interior design, as the pressure to be safe and stylish has taken grip. Consumer-friendly somehow translates into beige and brown. Young urban Asians are terrified that their house may look like a restaurant or, heaven forbid, a temple. Only the Hindus remain faithful to colour.

There are many modernist gardeners, however, who use colour well. Raymond Jungles (influenced by Roberto Burle Marx) is not shy of introducing a pistachio green wall or a mustard accent. Ng Sek San of Malaysia unleashes a riot of rich Malay colour in the lighting of his gardens. Bill Bensley introduces rich, almost Rajasthani, earth tones to many of his gardens, seen in his gate and wall designs and his planting schemes.

Tropical plants such as bougainvilleas, cordylines, codiaeums, water lilies, heliconias and gingers all come in a range of colours, including the truly spectacular. Bright tropical flowers are one of the joys of modern life.

Restraint needs to be exercised, however, in the choice of colours. Colours should match the exterior architecture and the hardscape; colour schemes must not be uncomfortable to the eye. A good guide when designing a modern tropical garden is to use brightly coloured ground covers and vines as backdrops, with brightly hued plants for the occasional accent. Using shades of green — from deep dark jungle green to phosphorescent lime green — can enrich a garden design with tonal variety.

ABOVE, TOP: Bright pink garden walls and Red Hot Cat's Tail (*Acalypha hispida*) flowers make for a vibrant clash of colour in this Mexican hotel garden.

ABOVE: Bromeliads come in a rich variety of shapes, and their foliage presents in a wide variety of patterns and colours. Many varieties have variegated leaves, while others may be spotted or have different colours on the tops and bottoms of the leaves. The variation seen in bromeliads can be used to create stunning colour accents, as in this Davis Dalbok-designed garden in Hilo, Hawaii.

FACING PAGE: *Lagerstroemia* casts a pink glow over its metal-clad partner, the building — the Disney Concert Hall in L.A., designed by Frank Gehry.

ABOVE: Timoteo Wachter planned a modern garden with *Pritchardia* palms as accents for the Ricardo Legorreta-designed house in Mexico.

FACING PAGE: Colourful, cosy corner — fresh and invigorating — in a small Miami backyard. The violent colour contrast starts with the garden wall and continues through the furniture.

ABOVE LEFT: This garden in Santa
Barbara, California is visually
anchored by a vivid blue wall.

ABOVE RIGHT: Walled courtyards are
best peopled with pots or furniture.

FACING PAGE: A licorice allsorts
accent stairway at Isabel
Goldsmith's Las Alamandas near
Careyes, Mexico.

Furniture

'They've got the furniture in the garden, and the plants in the house!!' Dame Edna Everage once famously said. Over the past decade, there has been a significant lifestyle change — homeowners had begun to spend all of their free time outdoors and needed durable furniture that they could keep outside. Advances in technology helped furniture designers to meet this demand. Gone are the days when a clunky pair of Adirondack chairs facing a kidney-shaped pool was considered modern. Gone too are the days when poolside or terrace furniture had to be carted in and out of storage.

Webbed aluminium furniture was a godsend and a new industry was created. This was especially so in Hawaii, where, during the same era, lanai-style housing — with large loggia and shaded terraces for entertaining and dining — called for a seamless match between indoor (or undercover) furniture and outdoor furniture. A thousand deco-inspired rattan chairs flooded the market.

Today, garden furniture and fabrics are designed for tropical conditions — for the heat and the intense ultraviolet light. Fabrics such as Sunbrella resist fading, while seat cushion foam has been redesigned to be totally porous. This gives water a chance to flow through the fabric. Even wicker is now reproduced in durable, almost undetectable plastic.

A crisp setting of modern garden furniture can add zest to an otherwise dull patio or terrace, and transform it into a useable space. Double sun-chairs, hooded cabana chairs (the Denon furniture company designed a

PAGE 134: The promenade at Pondicherry in India: Soviet-era social realism meets salt spray.

LEFT: The Avalon Hotel was renovated by Australian architects Koning Eizenberg and decorated by Kelly Wearstler. It overlooks Beverly Hills, California.

RIGHT: Chair lamp created from glass mosaic and fibreglass by Bali-based designer Dolf Sareli.

classic in the 1990s) and hammocks have replaced aluminium banana chairs and pastel painted rattan or cane lounge sets in the modern tropical garden. These are spaces which are now as much for chilling out and nodding off as they are for the consumption of iced lemon tea.

Care must be taken, however, that the garden does not end up looking like a furniture showroom, or an operating theatre. Clinical modernism — immensely popular with young professionals — can look chilling in a tropical garden setting. Garden designers should control the spatial orientation in a garden, as interior designers do in homes, but on the outside. The advice of interior designers should be sought in the design, shape and style of garden furniture, but the finished look — a garden that is well-balanced, between the natural and the man-made — is the landscape designer's responsibility.

A lot can be learned from looking at the way those in the Mediterranean use outdoor spaces in the summer — when life moves outside. There, vine-covered pergolas shade outdoor dining tables while cosy wicker chairs create seating groups for reading and outdoor conversation.

The Spanish Colonial style suburbs of Los Angeles provide an example of how outdoor spaces can be adapted. In the real estate boom years that followed the Second World War, swimming pools were added to the outdoor suburban living environment, creating a whole new living zone. Mexican architect Ricardo Legorreta includes outdoor furniture in the architecture of his exterior spaces, creating seating within walls or as a continuation of his outdoor terraces.

Today tropical homeowners and hotel visitors alike want the full range of outdoor entertainment and relaxation opportunities. Outdoor bars, BBQ areas, massage tents, tiki lights, outdoor speakers, meditation chambers, hammocks, waterbeds, and jacuzzis are all desired in tropical gardens and need to be designed in.

ABOVE: A modernist take on an Indian swing bed.

LEFT: Comfy, practical poolside button chair at The Park Hotel, Visakhapatnam, India.

FACING PAGE: Hammocks are the traditional outdoor furniture of Mexican gardens. Their steep parabolic curve always looks modern.

FACING PAGE: White Lotus and Jasmine arrangement viewed through a love donut (hole in spa table).

ABOVE LEFT: A large bunch of Lily of the Valley looks statuesque and modern in any setting.

ABOVE RIGHT: The much copied bronze vase designed by Ed Tuttle for The Sukhothai Hotel in Bangkok, here with a simple arrangement of creeping *Philodendron* leaves and flowers.

Striking modern floral displays using palm seeds, Heliconia flowers, white Pampas Grass, red *Anthurium*, *Cordyline* leaves, and *Plumeria* flowers. For a modern look, the vases are kept simple.

Roberto Burle Marx

FACING PAGE: Roberto Burle Marx's famous Copacabana promenade design — a perfect ploy for the Brazilian beach scene.

BELOW: Burle Marx loved Aztec ruinscapes, and he often worked them into his gardens as feature walls covered in plants, adjacent to water gardens also packed with plants.

In South America the artist and landscape designer Roberto Burle Marx, born in 1909 and a contemporary of Isamu Noguchi and Luis Barragán, introduced early modernist design into the Latin American landscape. Burle Marx was known for a sense of humour in both his work and life, calling himself a 'Burlesque Marxist', referring perhaps to the colourful free formalism of his work. 'I can largely explain my approach to design as the impact on my generation of cubism and abstractionism,' Burle Marx once said. His best known gardens are Flamingo Park in Rio de Janeiro, and the Copacabana beachfront with its ribbon of red, black and white mosaic waves adapted from an old 17th-century decorative pavement found in Lisbon (*see picture on left*).

Throughout his career Burle Marx alternated public and private commissions. One of the grandest of the latter was begun in 1946 for the Monteiro estate in Petropolis (*see plan of the garden on page 194*), a mountain resort north of Rio. 'For the first time, he was able to make a coherent statement using his two passions: the exotic plants of Brazil and the power of modernist art,' wrote garden historian Jamie James.

Burle Marx thought like an artist: 'A garden is the result of an arrangement of natural materials according to aesthetic laws, interwoven throughout are the artist's outlook on life, his past experiences, his affections, his attempts, his mistakes and his successes.' He was influenced as a child by his Brazilian mother who loved gardening and his German father's interest in design. At the age of 19, he went to Berlin to study painting, before continuing his studies in Rio de Janeiro at the School of Fine Arts, headed by influential architect Lucio Costa, who gave him his first commission, a small rooftop garden.

While in Germany, he discovered the Dahlem Botanical Garden which had a large collection of rare Brazilian tropical plants, and was inspired to approach garden design as abstract paintings, some curvilinear and some rectilinear, using native Brazilian plants to create blocks of colour. Burle Marx constantly invigorated his landscape designs with his artistic work. He was incredibly prolific, designing tiles and tapestries, as well as producing paintings and lithographs.

In 1949, he bought a small farm, now known as Sitio Burle Marx, about 45 km from Rio. This became his home and his studio. A long low house with a verandah overlooking a rectangular pool was the centre of a bustling nursery where he kept his tropical plant collection, one of the most important in the world. Fazenda Vargem Grande in Sao Paulo is typical of his later garden work. Water, particularly its music and sound, was important. Using water plants from all over the world, he created a vast garden with 200-foot terraces filled with pools and cascades forming sculptural sheets of water.

Outside of Brazil his reputation grew with commissions in Argentina, Los Angeles, Santiago de Chile, and the Brazilian Embassy in Washington. By his death in 1994, he had designed nearly 3000 gardens over a span of 60 years.

Bill Bensley

FACING PAGE: Bensley Design Studio created handsome classic Indian artworks for their makeover of the Hyderabad Marriott Hotel, India. Bill Bensley also did the exterior architecture which frames his artwork gardens.

LEFT: Bill Bensley is a ravishing draughtsman.

BELOW: His garden art is always whimsical, like this statue at The Oberoi, Mauritius.

Bill Bensley was born in Anaheim, California, the home of Disneyland, a fact which may or may not have had a bearing on his brilliant future career producing theatrical, fantasy landscapes.

He shot out of Harvard in 1978, 'like a shooting star,' said his classmate and fellow landscaper Karl Princic, and was soon apprenticed to the world's largest tropical landscape architecture firm, Belt Collins International, working from their Singapore office. Bensley soon earned a reputation in the tropical landscape world as a ravishing draughtsman and art-lover. Bensleyan accents started popping up in the region's larger gardens like raisin toast from a well-oiled Westinghouse.

On his first trip to Bali, in 1983 — to work with P.T. Wijaya on a residential project — his jaw was agape as he registered the potential of Indonesia's million artisans and stone carvers. Like a Cindy Sherman tank he quickly rolled over to P.T. Wijaya and secured an important commission for Belt Collins to work with Wijaya on the new Bali Hyatt pool. Wijaya provided the art and style consultancy for the project in the concept stage — Bensley's first pass of temple gates and dragon bridges was deemed too clichéd — and pointed Bensley down the garden path of ruinscapes and subtle landscape follies. It is a path Bensley has never left, some say, while adding, at every turn, his trademark artworks and follies. And many turns there have been: in the Indian Ocean, Egypt, Rajasthan, Hainan (China) as well as his home base, Thailand.

Bensley is at heart a showman and a modernist, with a classicalist's passion and training. His landscapes are poetic and natural, and teeming with cultural reference. If at times they appear over-embellished, they are always full of robust horticultural enthusiasm. His gardens are for fun and for exploration. They are very popular, understandably, with children.

In 2000 Bensley collaborated on a book with Singaporean architect-writer Tan Hock Beng called *Tropical Paradise* which featured Bensley's stunning photos of his own work and reproductions of magnificent airbrush drawings from his office.

Bruce Goold

Bruce Goold is a designer based in Sydney whose work — landscape design, graphic design and interior decorating — is inspired by the exotic tropics. His studio-home and garden in Palm Beach, Sydney's most gorgeous suburb, is something of a museum of tropical decorative arts — rattan, bamboo, tropical textile prints — as well as a think tank for lovers of tropicalia.

His lamps, fountains, verandah furniture designs and textile designs are unique in today's tropical world as they continue the tradition of the 1950s Hawaiian designers, who look intensely at nature when searching for inspiration.

His interiors always look exterior somehow. And his verandah designs — *South Pacific meets From Here to Eternity* — are eclectic and whimsical. Like Oliver Messel, another great tropical 'decorator' of the second half of the 20th century, Goold improvises with shells and sharks' eggs and *objets trouvés* when creating a new living environment. Less structured or classical than Messel or Cecil Beaton, Goold infuses his work with a sense of whimsy, and the surreal. The modest studio-home he shares with his wife Katie is not enough to contain the outpouring of his decorative ideas — expressed as tablescapes, floral tributes and tropical settings — so he rotates the furniture and art constantly. To visit the studio-home monthly would be to experience a kaleidoscope of decorative magic. Hopefully someday soon a clever developer will let Goold loose on a small tropical island with a big palace so he can satiate his artistic skills.

In 1998 P.T. Wijaya collaborated with Goold on a few designs for our Tropical Shop in Bali. In 2003 we worked together on the garden artwork and graphic for a hotel in Pacific Harbour, Fiji. In 2004 Goold was roped in to design china-mosaic murals for our garden at the Taj Wellington Mews apartments in Mumbai. Goold impressed all who worked with him with his artistic sensibility and *joie de vivre*.

FACING PAGE: Original artwork by Bruce Goold used as mural art on the china-mosaic walls at the Taj Wellington Mews apartments, Mumbai, India.

RIGHT: Bruce and Katie Goold's living room in their Palm Beach, Sydney studio-home. Picture on far right is a detail of a screen print by Bruce Goold.

Chang Huai-Yan

FACING PAGE: Chang Huai-Yan's office garden, Singapore, 2003. The ideas in this garden are sort of old but Huai-Yan gives them a fresh modernist twist.

BELOW: Huai-Yan's design of a lily pond in urban Singapore. This clever design combines living plant walls with rustic-edged formality.

Chang Huai-Yan was a student of mine at the School of Architecture, National University of Singapore. He distinguished himself by sitting still and silent through an absolutely gripping five terms of lecturing.

At the end-of-the-year party in 1996, we were watching a miniature train set go around a miniature of the university campus when the class pushed Huai-Yan forward and he nervously showed me his diary-style sketchbook. The sketches were amazing — artistic, poetic, masterly — and I quickly booked him to do the artist impressions for *Tropical Garden Design*, the companion volume to this book.

During the course of our working relationship in Bali, he struck up a friendship with photographer Tim Street-Porter and his artist wife Annie Kelly. They encouraged Huai-Yan to experiment with making gardens, while pursuing a career in architectural design. In 1999 he worked with my office and Fairuz Salleh of Pacific-Nature Landscapes, and decided to concentrate on landscape not architectural design. He quickly learned the ropes and, in 2002, quietly set up a design office, Salad Dressing, with a few friends in the Singapore suburbs.

Huai-Yan has since earned a reputation as a romantic modernist with an artistic touch. The company works mainly in Singapore, but has also done gardens in Bali, Malaysia and Japan. His gardens are like his drawings — simple, pure and poetic. He likes to use accent palms and ferns in dialogue with striking artworks or big rocks. They are more than conversation pieces, however, as they invite the viewer to ponder. Like good poetry. His own office in Singapore — in a 1970s duplex home — is a clever reworking of the L.A. tropical style with lots of fun furniture and an outdoor entertaining area.

Huai-Yan travels extensively throughout tropical Asia sketching the world as he looks for inspiration for his gardens. He also combines illustration with garden design by drawing life-size botanical based murals. This allows him to escape into his own fictional gardens.

Jamie Durie

Garden designer Jamie Durie started humbly — as a sexy dancer and circus acrobat, in *Manpower* and *Cirque du Soleil*, respectively. He then combined his good looks and good taste on a television show, *Backyard Blitz*, a garden makeover series in which plain suburban backyards were turned into smart, outdoor living rooms. His design company, Patio, is almost singlehandedly responsible, through the popular television programme and a series of books, for a boom of backyard blitzes of the interlocking entertainment court variety in all of Australia, just as stringent water restrictions were making leafy gardens of the traditional variety almost a thing of the past.

Sri Lanka-born Durie spent most of his formative years looking around Southeast Asia (and not Europe, as had been the tradition up until the 1970s) for inspiration. His designs are most influenced perhaps by the tropical Asian modernist styles rather than the Australian modern garden which tends to use palettes of Australian native plants and favours a more unstructured look. Occasionally his work exhibits decorative touches from his Sri Lankan heritage.

Patio's signature style can be considered architectural, contemporary subtropical, with a twist of New Asia. Durie's gardens are leafy and quirky, but really they are about functionality and structure. In his book *Patio*, he explains that 'it's important to make a garden people-friendly and set up for living outdoors.'

Durie likes to play with timber and stone elements — as accent artworks and as artfully crafted hardscape elements. His outdoor furniture, generally built into stone paved courts or cantilevered from feature walls, is bold and masculine in the Australian beach-side tradition. His planting schemes are sometimes soft and caressing, sometimes bold and brash, to go with the 'standout' quality of his courtyard designs. Palms, tree ferns and alocasias are principal players in his outdoor stage sets. The result: garden designs which are trendy, fresh, and ultimately photographable (like Durie himself).

Durie now hosts *Dancing with the Stars* with Torvill and Dean while designing gardens all over the world.

FACING PAGE: Bold, sculptural forms and stripes are a recurring theme in many of Australian modernist Jamie Durie's work. Wild river grasses and ferns help to soften the 'architecture' in the garden.

LEFT: Jamie Durie of Patio likes to fuse the boundary between industrial art and garden design. This showpiece garden has innovative, caged granite boulder wall segments which are a surreal juxtaposition to the feathery desert 'Black Boy' cycads.

Karl Princic

Karl Princic is the quiet achiever in the Southeast Asian landscape design world. He started his career in California and Hawaii before being employed by Belt Collins International in 1984 to work in their Singapore office — with Bill Bensley. While with Belt Collins, he took on the InterContinental Bali Resort at Jimbaran Bay, the nearby Amanusa, and the adjacent villas and golf club, all with the architectural firm Kerry Hill Architects.

On these early jobs he showed an artful natural touch with his gentle, Hawaii-lite tropical softscapes. He also became a deft hand with handsome structured architectonic hardscapes, influenced, one imagines, by

his work with Kerry Hill, and this would characterise his Bali work from then on.

In 1990, he left Belt Collins and set up his own practice in Sanur, Bali, where he flourished. His work in Jakarta during the 1990s was elegant and sophisticated, particularly that done on the extensive grounds of The Dharmawangsa hotel and The Pakubuwono apartments. Princic blended a Hawaiian sense for the natural-tropical with the Javanese courtyard style.

In 1999, he was invited to do the gardens for the ultra-modern The Balé in Nusa Dua, Bali, working side by side with confirmed minimalist architect Antony Liu from Jakarta, and landscape contractor I Ketut Marsa (formerly of Marsa and Wijaya) with whom Princic struck up a great working relationship. Princic's gardens for The Balé are minimalist with a restricted plant palette, but definitely magical. Through mass planting of wild grasses and spider lilies, he managed to soften the tank-trap style of the architecture.

Since then Princic has worked with a number of modernists: with Cheong Yew Kuan on the Begawan Giri Estate in Bali (now hotelier Christina Ong's Como Shambhala Estate); with Antony Liu again on The Oasis on Benoa Bay, Bali; as well as on many other residential projects with Bali's burgeoning stable of modernist architects.

Princic's style can perhaps be defined by that of his own home and studio in Sanur — crisp and uncluttered, almost clinical, but demonstrating a master's understanding of how to successfully blend modern architecture with landscape elements.

FACING PAGE: A handsome corner of Princic's own garden in his Bali studio-home. Strong architectural forms are teamed with soft feathery grasses and trees.

LEFT: Princic's hardscapes and pondscapes at The Balé in Bali are bold and masculine.

Martin Palleros

Martin Palleros describes himself as a man from the pampas of Argentina. Soft-spoken and mild of manner, Palleros knows how to deliver a punch on the site — his landscape designs are dramatic, crisp and edgy.

An architect by training with master planning experience in large offices in Florida and California in the USA, Palleros burst onto the landscape design scene when he established Tierra Design in 1992 in Singapore and later Bangkok (after a long stint at a large architectural design office in Singapore).

His timing was excellent. His crossover into purely landscape design came at the start of the minimalist New Asia movement and he soon received important commissions from top architects Ernesto Bedmar and Kerry Hill (The Chedi Chiang Mai) and hotelier Christina Ong (the Metropolitan Bangkok).

Initially his landscape work, particularly for house gardens, was a tad heavy on the hardscape. He was to find his métier in the larger spaces of apartments and hotels where his more architectural finishes — his signature stone detailing and architectonic space planning — had room to breathe.

My favourite project is the Metropolitan Bangkok hotel gardens where his experience with plaza and institution design shows in the excellent space planning in the hotel's arrival courtyard. The blend of ribbed, rough-stone, light-grey granite paving, and fine-leafed tropical-alpine trees and grass, gives the area the feel of an arctic oasis in a sweaty city. The swimming pool, which can be viewed from the restaurant, is large, lined with blue-black Thai ceramic tiles. At night, blue and purple fibre optic lights create light patterns as the water ripples over an infinity edge.

Palleros's work for the riverside The Chedi Chiang Mai is exemplary. Palleros chose giant specimens of local *Ficus* — almost everything is available at the plant markets in Chiang Mai these days — and placed them boldly in the handsome courts and at the hotel entrance, a perfect foil for Kerry Hill's striking architecture. The swimming pool court is also elegant. Parallel to the river, the dark pool with a long infinity edge flank cascades into a long formal pond dotted, intentionally, with ordered clumps of vibrant water lilies.

Palleros now operates from a base in Perth where he has already garnered awards for his sleek and stylish landscape designs.

FACING PAGE: Pond design at The Chedi Chiang Mai.

LEFT: Stunning riverside bungalow and garden in Kanchanaburi, Thailand, designed by Martin Palleros.

Nancy Goslee Power

Nancy Goslee Power has worked on many gardens — for Frank Gehry, Rem Koolhaas and other internationally known architects. Based in Santa Monica, a beachside suburb of Los Angeles, she was originally an interior designer but turned to garden design in 1981.

Today, she could be considered California's best-known garden designer. She has an instinctive understanding of the abstract shapes of tropical and dry climate plants, and uses them in sophisticated colour combinations. Goslee Power has also travelled extensively around the world, including the tropics where she found much of her inspiration.

Los Angeles has arguably America's greatest collection of modernist residential architecture. It has a dry subtropical climate which, with added water, can sustain most tropical plants. The use of tropical-style planting — indoors and out — has added drama to the many modernist house designs in the area.

Goslee Power has said that to create a tropical garden in Los Angeles, it has to be lush and heavily planted. She advocates the use of palm trees and plants with fat luscious leaves. She also recommends the use of tree ferns which feel tropical. She believes in the importance of the sound of water in the garden and plenty of shade. Her favourite tropical garden in Los Angeles is the little known Virginia Robinson Gardens in Beverly Hills which have a wonderful collection of palms, both native and imported, primarily from Australia.

Goslee Power's own work can be seen at the Norton Simon Museum in Pasadena where she transformed the extensive sculpture garden using a mixture of native grasses and exotic trees from Asia.

She is not afraid of colour, and is inspired by the colours of nearby Latin America. Her most famous quote is: 'There is no such thing as an ugly coloured plant, it just depends on what colour you put next to it.'

FACING PAGE: The raised pond in the backyard of Goslee Power's cute Santa Monica, California cottage. The exaggerated edge and back board are softened by a weeping Angel's Trumpet (*Brugmansia*) and a healthy mix of water plants.

LEFT: This fountain at the Norton Simon Museum in Pasadena is made of Sierra granite.

Ng Sek San

FACING PAGE: Broad stairs cascade down a hillside towards the riverside pavilion entrance to the Bukit Gita Bayu resort, Malaysia.

BELOW: A severe, theatrical Sek San garden with dramatic lighting effect. Three lean trunks add nature to an otherwise man-made environment.

Ng Sek San is a Malaysian treasure. He loves his own culture, hates modern (commercial) *fengshui*, is a deft hand with environmental design, shouts from a soapbox about oppression in his industry (landscape design) and recycles! As his success has soared so has he modified his outfits, from Kiwi woodchuck — he studied and worked in New Zealand for 12 years — to grunge ninja. He is a very grounded guy. He likens his work to being a bit like organic farming — the carrots love tomatoes thing. It is about symbiosis; bricks love stones, steel beams love bottles, cacti love cages, rubble loves concrete vent blocks. The compositing really gets the flavour going — it is delicious.

He has kept his office small, despite his success, but manages to complete five or ten serious projects a year. His heroes are Charles Saatchi, Ernesto Che Guevara and Martha Schwartz (like many neo-Kiwis, he is only a bit confused). His gardens run from the joyously natural (Taman Warisan Apartments in Kuala Lumpur, Malaysia, where I first discovered his work) to the architectonic-anarchic. A frequent ploy is the use of industrial finishes (in a slightly irreverent way) but his gardens never look gimmicky. He gets his ideas from nature, from collaborating with the dynamic Malay and Chinese societies in which he lives, from working intimately with artisans and artists. And from his own activist-aesthetic warrior spirit.

He has a special genius for placing trees to create the ordered jungle look. His own studio home has a giant Indian Pulai Tree (*Alstonia scholaris*) in front of it. His is a self-professed free-range radical, and his gardens are beautifully detailed and executed even if they fly in the face of convention, as Sek San likes to put it.

Sek San's recent exhibit at the Malaysia International Landscape & Garden Festival 2006 is illustrative. Its very simplicity made it feel elitist even though it was a celebration of nature. Sek San avoided ruining the tender site by putting the built forms — decks and paths of perforated metal (the oil rig variety) — up on stilts which allowed the site to breathe. There were walls made of 'cages' of dried leaves. In the middle of the installation was an elegant white squat toilet, with Martha Stewart toilet paper. It raised many socialist eyebrows. Ng Sek San definitely challenges the parameters of his profession, in a nice wholesome way.

Martin Palleros

Martin Palleros describes himself as a man from the pampas of Argentina. Soft-spoken and mild of manner, Palleros knows how to deliver a punch on the site — his landscape designs are dramatic, crisp and edgy.

An architect by training with master planning experience in large offices in Florida and California in the USA, Palleros burst onto the landscape design scene when he established Tierra Design in 1992 in Singapore and later Bangkok (after a long stint at a large architectural design office in Singapore).

His timing was excellent. His crossover into purely landscape design came at the start of the minimalist New Asia movement and he soon received important commissions from top architects Ernesto Bedmar and Kerry Hill (The Chedi Chiang Mai) and hotelier Christina Ong (the Metropolitan Bangkok).

Initially his landscape work, particularly for house gardens, was a tad heavy on the hardscape. He was to find his métier in the larger spaces of apartments and hotels where his more architectural finishes — his signature stone detailing and architectonic space planning — had room to breathe.

My favourite project is the Metropolitan Bangkok hotel gardens where his experience with plaza and institution design shows in the excellent space planning in the hotel's arrival courtyard. The blend of ribbed, rough-stone, light-grey granite paving, and fine-leafed tropical-alpine trees and grass, gives the area the feel of an arctic oasis in a sweaty city. The swimming pool, which can be viewed from the restaurant, is large, lined with blue-black Thai ceramic tiles. At night, blue and purple fibre optic lights create light patterns as the water ripples over an infinity edge.

Palleros's work for the riverside The Chedi Chiang Mai is exemplary. Palleros chose giant specimens of local *Ficus* — almost everything is available at the plant markets in Chiang Mai these days — and placed them boldly in the handsome courts and at the hotel entrance, a perfect foil for Kerry Hill's striking architecture. The swimming pool court is also elegant. Parallel to the river, the dark pool with a long infinity edge flank cascades into a long formal pond dotted, intentionally, with ordered clumps of vibrant water lilies.

Palleros now operates from a base in Perth where he has already garnered awards for his sleek and stylish landscape designs.

FACING PAGE: Pond design at The Chedi Chiang Mai.

LEFT: Stunning riverside bungalow and garden in Kanchanaburi, Thailand, designed by Martin Palleros.

Raymond Jungles

FACING PAGE: Raymond Jungles loves coloured cement paths, here used in a Florida garden.

BELOW: A signature Raymond Jungles garden with a clever mix of geometric and natural forms. This stunning jungle pool, with attached lay-easy area (called a sea-cow mating ledge in the trade) was realised for clients in Panama.

Raymond Jungles has worked extensively in Florida, the southernmost state of the USA, and the only mainland state that could truly be called tropical. It is a mostly flat peninsula without mountains or hills to give scale to the landscape. 'We don't have the drama of mountains in South Florida, we have clouds,' explains Jungles, 'and my gardens are about contrasting textures.'

Jungles was an architecture student when he met Roberto Burle Marx at a lecture he gave at the University of Florida. That was in 1977. Burle Marx inspired the young student to switch to landscape design, even inviting Jungles to Brazil. A new world opened up for him as he accompanied the distinguished landscape designer on expeditions into the tropical forests of Brazil in search of rare and new plants.

In the 1990s, while working from a Key West, Florida base, he completed numerous enchanting gardens in the backyards of modest Key West homes. The signature Jungles tropical colours in hardscape emerged as he honed his softscaping skills. In Jungles' view, the light in the tropics is usually more intense, so a lot of colour can be used. 'There are many plants that have an integral colour that is permanent that can be used against a coloured hardscape element such as a wall,' Jungles adds.

Modernist architectural elements such as low retaining walls, angular walkways and Burle Marxist style murals provide counterpoints to his naturalist massing of plants. Jungles is one of the few modernists who prefer gentler softscapes to caress the harsher edges of his hardscapes. Florida native pines and grasses are generally mixed into artful natural, but vibrant, planting schemes.

One of his more sensational gardens in the Coral Gables area south of Miami consists of interlocking ravines blown out of the limestone bedrock of a garden-loving couple's backyard. It is very dramatic and theatrical — a veritable Tarzan film set, complete with waterfalls and waterholes — but naturalistic. Jungles chose to keep the local pine and tufty grass bushland running through the planting scheme, which has occasional non-intrusive accents.

In his Naples and Miami area residential work — which tends to be on a grand scale — Jungles mixes the client's need for horticultural attractions with his own love for the 'Burlesque Marxist'. He combines gravel drives and nature walks with dramatic paved courts and water features. He is currently working on a Brazilian Garden for the Naples Botanical Garden in Florida — a homage to his mentor Roberto Burle Marx.